NEW APPRECIATIONS IN
HISTORY 16

British Women in the Nineteenth Century

by Dorothy K.G. Thompson

D1407369

The Historical Association

59a Kennington Park Road, London SE11 4JH

Front and back covers: *Punch* (1849)

ACKNOWLEDGEMENTS

The pictures on pages 8 and 10 are reproduced by permission of the Mary Evans Picture Library.

The picture on page 12 is reproduced by permission of the British Library.

The picture on page 20 is reproduced by courtesy of The Dickens House.

The picture on page 21 is reproduced by permission of the BBC Hulton Picture Library.

The picture on page 26 is reproduced by permission of The Museum of London.

The picture on page 29 is reproduced by permission of the Master and Fellows of Trinity College Cambridge

The picture on page 30 is reproduced by permission of the Syndics of Cambridge University Library.

This pamphlet has been edited by J.M. Bourne

The Historical Association, founded in 1906, brings together people who share an interest in, and love for, the past. It aims to further the study and teaching of history at all levels: teacher and student, amateur and professional. This is one of over 100 publications available at very preferential rates to members. Membership also includes journals at generous discounts and gives access to courses, conferences, tours and regional and local activities. Full details are available from The Secretary, The Historical Association, 59a Kennington Park Road, London SE11 4JH, telephone: 01-735 3901

The publication of a pamphlet by the Historical Association does not necessarily imply the Association's approval of the opinions expressed in it.

© Dorothy K.G. Thompson, 1989, reprinted 1992, reprinted with revisions, 1993

Designed and prepared by Colin Barker, MCSD

Originated and published by The Historical Association, 59a Kennington Park Road, London SE11 4JH and printed in Great Britain by The Chameleon Press Limited, 5-25 Burr Road, London SW18 4SG

2

Contents

British Women in the Nineteenth Century

A short pamphlet surveying the historical record of rather more than half the population of Britain over a period of a hundred years must of necessity be sketchy and incomplete. The great interest in the history of women which has arisen in the last few decades has produced a great deal of lively and stimulating work, but in many crucial areas there is still a good deal of controversy while in others there is more speculation and guesswork than scholarly investigation. This survey looks at work that has been done on some of the most important questions that concerned women in Britain during the last century, and suggests possible further reading. It can, however, only deal with a small selection of the many works available.

By British women I mean women living in the British Isles. By the end of the nineteenth century there were many millions of women throughout the Empire who were British, but their history is outside the scope of this survey. In the British Isles there were hundreds of thousands of women in areas of Ireland, Scotland and Wales who did not speak English and whose history is still for the most part only sketchily written, if at all. I have decided, however, not to restrict discussion to England alone, if only to indicate the need for more consideration of the lives of women in the regions and nations. Laws in Ireland and Scotland differed in some ways from those in England and Wales, language, dialect and customs differed greatly from region to region.

Nevertheless, the British Isles were governed by the same central institutions, and the movements of population which took place during the century meant that the regions, although retaining great differences, were never totally cut off from each other. Millions of Welsh, Highland and Irish women moved to the cities to work, whilst the wealthier landowning and commercial classes had social and business connections which cut across national and regional boundaries.

The questions which historians and their readers ask of the past are usually related to the preoccupations of their own generation. It is hardly surprising that the twentieth century, which has seen the arrival in Britain of a political system in which every citizen over the age of eighteen has a parliamentary vote, has also seen a great interest in nineteenth century movements for the extension of the franchise. The admission of women to the exercise of the vote has been achieved in the present century, and the history of the individuals, movements and journals that campaigned for this achievement has been extensively studied and recorded.[1] Since the 1960s, however, a new women's movement has arisen — perhaps better described as a number of movements — concerned with much wider questions of women's place in society than political and parliamentary rights. The recognition that exclusion from political activity was only one of the forms of inequality experienced by women has led to a great flowering of research into the past and present social position of women and into the ideas and beliefs that supported that position. Most publishers now have a list of publications specifically concerned with women, indeed the length of such lists is daunting to the ordinary reader. Fortunately a number of excellent bibliographies exist, and these, together with the suggestions for further reading contained in most of the books which are mentioned here, should be consulted for more extended study.[2]

The student of the history of women faces problems of definition and vocabulary which are probably greater than those involved in most other areas of history. Different schools and different authors endow words with different meanings. Some words which are commonly used still do not bear agreed definitions. It is necessary, therefore, to look at one or two of the more problematic or contentious of these.

To begin with, there may be differences of perception between those who concern themselves with the history of women and those who are concerned with women's history. The latter expression is often, though by no means invariably, used by those who believe that women perceive things differently from men, express themselves differently and teach and learn differently. In extreme cases this may mean that courses are offered in women's history from which male students and books by men are excluded.

Another semantic problem for students and writers of the history of women lies in the varied uses of the word 'patriarchy'. Some feminist writers now use the word to describe any system of society in which men are the more powerful and dominant sex. The older meaning of rule by the father has been displaced by the simpler one of gender- domination. This rules out the questions of inter- generational relations contained in the traditional use of the word and leaves only gender relations. There is certainly a problem here in that there seems no single word to describe all male-dominated societies, but not every one is happy about the contraction of the concept of patriarchy into this more simple meaning.[3]

A third question which has emerged in recent writing about sex-roles in society is the distinction between 'sex' and 'gender'. There is less confusion here than in the other two cases, although there is not complete consistency in the use of the two words. In general the word 'sex' is used when speaking of the biological descriptions of men and women, while 'gender' refers to the social roles or the norms and expectations of behaviour on the part of men and women which occur in particular societies. Thus one society may consider agricultural work to be female while another regards such work as entirely male, to use a simple example. A problem with this distinction, which is a very necessary one for the consideration of the history of men and women in society, is that until recently the word 'gender' was used entirely as a grammatical term. The more modern usage does not exclude the grammatical sense, but it will rarely if ever be found in its wider meaning during the nineteenth century. Writers like Mary Wollstonecraft use the word 'sex' to cover both meanings.[4]

There are other problems involved in the projection of modern concerns back into the study of the past. It may be very stimulating to re-examine the past in terms of our modern ideas, and can lead to clarity and understanding. It can also be confusing and may lead to serious mis-readings, especially if terms and concepts are applied out of context and not consistent with the contemporary usage. The need for a close and contextual examination of documents and other historical sources is nowhere of greater importance than in studying the history of women. Words which once had a meaning which included both sexes — words such as 'mob', 'crowd', 'apprentice' and many others, came to be interpreted in the course of the nineteenth century as entirely male. Schools founded in earlier centuries for the education of 'poor children' were revived in the Victorian period as boys' schools, and the history of popular movements in

the early nineteenth century — to quote only one example of the process — was distorted by the interpretation placed by later historians on these hitherto inclusive words. Language, spoken and written, is an important source for the recovery of the past, but as a source for the history of women, it has always to be studied in context.

'Public and Private' — the World of Ideas

The nineteenth century saw an unprecedented expansion in the volume of all kinds of printed matter in Britain. Books, journals, newspapers and pamphlets poured from the presses. Very much of this material was written by women, even more was written for and was read by women. Any one who has read at all widely in the literature and other writing of the century knows that there is no more uniformity among women writers than among men. Women as different from each other as Hannah More, Jane Austen, Maria Edgeworth, the Brontë sisters, George Eliot, Elizabeth Gaskell, Mrs Humphrey Ward and Eliza Lynn Linton have left a rich variety of works of fiction, learned articles, journalism and other published material, as well as unpublished journals and letters. The very scale of this literary heritage led many early writers about women to lean heavily and somewhat uncritically on it as a way of understanding women's lives. An example might be the extremely dismal picture of the lives of Victorian governesses which was drawn from the lives and writings of the Brontës. But although the works of women of genius and talent are extremely illuminating, it has to be remembered that such women were set aside from most of their sex by their talent and by their exceptional life-experience. Outstanding women who were public figures in their lifetimes are a part of the story, but only a very small part. For most women life was private and family-

based, and their experiences are far less accessible.

The lives of outstanding women have been studied, and continue to be of interest. In general, though, the history of the political and public life of the nation is the history of men. Historians seeking to recover the private and family life of the majority of women have had to look for sources other than state papers and the political press. The nineteenth century saw the development of an ideology of separate spheres of activity for the sexes — public for men and private for women. The public world of politics, the market and the workplace was the location of rough, competitive male activities, while the private world of home and family encapsulated the Christian virtues and the morality of personal relationships. The belief that this was a necessary division was held by many women as well as men, and was, for example, used against the advocates of women's suffrage by those who contended that the public world was by definition coarsening and corrupting. The philosophical lineage of this idea has been examined in an interesting study by Jean Bethke Elshtain. It is not possible to understand the changes which took place in women's status and the controversies surrounding the changes without taking account of this concept.[5]

The ideology of separate spheres was very much that of an influential section of middle class opinion. The option of so dividing their lives was rarely open to working people, among whom neither access to the world of politics nor the possibility of a domestic world

untrammelled by the need to take paid work outside the home were for the majority ever attainable. The family responsibilities were certainly generally divided between the husband as bread-winner and the wife as home-maker, and it usually seems to have fallen to the women to bind the family with the ties of care and affection, but for the poor there was neither public authority nor private seclusion. Among women of the wealthiest families choices had always been more open, but by the middle years of the century there seems to have been a remarkable degree of acceptance of the separate spheres ideology among all strata of the upper classes, at least until the

emergence in the last decades of the 'new woman' and all that she stood for. It should, however, always be remembered that for the last two-thirds of the century the highest position in the land was held by a woman who combined in her life and person the public and the private roles. Queen Victoria was the first monarch in modern times of whom this could be said. She came to the throne unmarried, chose as consort a man who was her social inferior and who never equalled her in rank or status, whose name she never assumed and who never acquired the rights over his wife's property to which all other husbands among her subjects laid claim under the law of coverture . For most of her life she took an active part in the public political life of the country, but at the same time played the role of a devoted and conscientious mother to her large family.[6]

It is clear then that the ideas which seemed to be held in a general way throughout Victorian society about the relative status and roles of men and women turn out, on closer examination, to have been interpreted very differently in different classes. Indeed, the more one examines the lives of actual women and the expectations and constraints under which they lived and worked, the more problematic does the division between 'public' and 'private' appear. It persisted, however, as an essential element in nineteenth century thought.

Modern research and writing has brought into question a number of assumptions which underlay nineteenth century women's movements and the earlier writing about them. The first studies of movements for women's emancipation tended to see a century opening in the dark ages of the total subjection of women and gradually moving towards the daylight of liberation in the very last years. Recent work has modified this view. Some writers now suggest that in a nation in which the majority of the population lived outside large conurbations, where small family farms, domestic industrial workshops and family businesses were still the most

numerous forms of working units, work was generally family-based and, although jobs might be gender-specific, there was more overlap and certainly more mutual understanding of work and business within the family. In some of the professions and crafts, too, where the work was carried on from home, women, especially widows and unmarried daughters, might carry on what was normally men's work if the man of the family was ill,

overworked or absent. The development of large-scale industry, the 'professionalisation' of occupations and the pastoralisation of the countryside led to a situation in the middle decades of the century in which the possibilities of interesting and well-paid work for women actually declined, at least relatively. For middle- and upper-class women this could mean that their lives were more exclusively home-centred and basically frivolous (provided the husband's income allowed for a reasonable number of servants) while for women of the working class it could mean that work to supplement their husband's wage or to replace it if he was not working, became less and less skilled, increasingly casual and badly paid.

The changes which were taking place in the location and organisation of work during the nineteenth century were accompanied by the movement of large numbers of people into towns and cities. For many the anonymity and the greater opportunities for employment in towns provided a welcome escape from the supervision of squire, parson and neighbours in the rural community. But for women in particular the escape from neighbourhood supervision could lead to greater exploitation in work and to the loss of family support in marriage. The life of the very poor was harsh in any circumstance, but there is evidence to suggest that the pollution of the environment combined with exploitative practices by tradespeople, whether the adulteration of food or the extortionate terms of credit trading, and with the increasingly casual nature

Queen Victoria

This picture of the Royal Family at Osborne, taken in 1859, is an example of the strong projection of the family image with which she was always associated.

The Queen's Consort, 'or the Queen Consort.---Which?

A PROSPECTION OF THREE WEEKS AFTER MARRIAGE.

Pray, Madam, am I not your lawful husband?

Well, sir—then am I not your lord and *master!* (Query, sir.—It cannot be disputed, madam, and I say again that I WILL have a considerable increase to my income. What's a paltry £50,000 per annum, for a prince of my importance—that will hardly pay for my amusements. *I will* have another palace, too, and a couple of hunting villas to boot—and more than that, madam, I will interfere in the affairs of the state, and have considerable influence in the army also—and all in defiance of either you or old Jack Bull.

From Cleave's Penny Gazette of Variety and Amusements, Dec 7, 1839, more than two months before the royal wedding.

of urban employment meant that life for the poor in towns and cities could be even harder than it was for rural labourers. Certainly the conditions among casual workers in the cities, especially among women in sweated and out-working trades which were revealed by social investigators from Mayhew onwards, suggest a precariousness of existence and a degree of exploitation which could hardly have been worse.[7]

We may, therefore, see a social profile for the nineteenth century in which changes in the tempo, location and reward of work affected all classes. Larger units of work and larger concentrations of dwellings brought about changes in perceptions and in family relations. A shift in emphasis took place in the course of the century from the family to the individual as wage earner and vector of family skills and traditions and at the same time the growth of an ideology of competition and self-advancement left behind the unskilled worker or the worker whose skill was not marketable — including that of the woman trained in housework and child-rearing — since the most important form of recognition, monetary reward, was not for them.

Homes which were not also

workshops or counting houses were clearly more comfortable and more easily managed. This fact, combined with the growing idealisation of the home and of the woman as 'the angel in the house', may have made life better for many women. The cheerful nineteenth-century housewife with her nursery-full of cheerful children and her ready acceptance of the role of universal comforter of husband, children, servants and relatives must have existed and have relished the praise which she earned from moralists and divines. She has, however, found little place as yet in the historical record. It was surely to such as she that Mrs Beeton addressed her book of *Household Management* published in 1861. Mrs Beeton, however, felt constrained to write by the fact that so many husbands preferred their clubs to their homes for rest and refreshment. And the illustration with which the volume was prefaced was of a very pre-Victorian rural homestead flanked by a hay meadow and a farmyard. Samuel Butler, whose novel *The Way of All Flesh* gives one of the most critical accounts of the Victorian middle-class family in fiction, has his hero, Ernest Pontifex, settle his two children with a bargee to be brought up as members of the upper stratum of the working class. Booth, in his survey of London life, found this same stratum of the regularly employed and decently-paid artisans to be the happiest in society; he too compared their lives favourably with those of higher social groups. It may be that the women of this particular stratum had enough money coming in to provide a good clean home and nourishing meals for their family, enough work and more to fill their day and also the chance to use domestic skills to improve the life of all the family. But even for this class life was uncertain. Accident or illness or the falling-off of demand for the husband's skill could push the family rapidly into poverty and require the wife to augment their income by casual work. For the lower strata of the working class life was a continual struggle and the women rarely had the opportunity to devote themselves entirely to domestic pursuits. As women came to organise for greater freedom and more choice in their lives during the latter decades of the century, the inadequacy of the domestic role came increasingly to be highlighted.

Whatever satisfaction and fulfilment marriage provided for women, however, there still remained many for whom marriage and family were not options. Statistics show that in all classes there were more women than men, and women came increasingly to live longer than men as the century continued. Occupations available to women were limited by tradition and prejudice as well as by the masculinisation and professionalisation which effectively excluded women from training for most jobs by the second half of the century.

Many women and some more perceptive men recognised the extent to which women in nineteenth century Britain were treated as second class citizens. An important part of the history of the century is the story of the different campaigns and movements which took place to improve women's status and to give women — or in some cases to restore to them — some power over their own lives. These campaigns tended to take two main forms which are reflected in the women's movements of the nineteenth and twentieth centuries and also in recent work on the history of women. They are to some degree contradictory. On the one hand was the demand for the admission of women to the public sphere — for education and training for responsible work, for recognition of women's work and skills by more equal payment, for equality of political rights and legal status with men within marriage as well as outside. On the other hand was a demand for more recognition of the importance of the private sphere — for education in household management, domestic economy and child-rearing and the recognition of the work which most women were in fact doing every day, but for which they received no training and little recognition.

In the history which has been written, these two tendencies can be traced. Outstanding women who have led campaigns or produced great creative work have been the subjects of biographies, and the renewal of interest has led to the discovery of forgotten figures and to the reinterpretation of the lives of some of the well-known. Work of this kind has been done since the time of the women concerned. Information about women as a whole, however, or about the family during the nineteenth century has only recently attracted historians, and most of the work that has been done on these questions has appeared since about 1960.

Work and the Family

Modern writers have increasingly come to see that the work of women, whether married or not, has to be understood in relation to their place in the family. Men's work and women's work may often have consisted of identical tasks, but the social and legal conditions governing its performance and the reward given for it were based on a perception of the worker's family role. It is, for example, interesting that, although the century saw many reports on women's work and conditions of work, there were no reports on the two occupations — domestic service and laundry work — which employed the largest number of women until the very end of the century. Such work was seen by the potential investigators as a natural extension of women's family role; indeed the nineteenth

Frontispiece to *Beeton's Book of Household Management* edited by Mrs Isabella Beeton.

century usage of the word 'family' usually included servants. What was seen as a social problem was the presence of women in work outside the home, and work in which they cooperated or competed with men. The experience of women as workers was one of the first questions to interest the generation of women scholars who entered the academic professions in the early years of the present century. Even where they were not concerned with women only, these women writers brought to their researches a new awareness of the presence of women.

The study by Ivy Pinchbeck of women's work during the industrial revolution was published as long ago as 1930. Modern scholars will not all agree with the underlying assumptions about the liberating effects of industrial employment on women, but nevertheless the book remains the standard work on the subject. As the author herself wrote in her preface to the 1969 reprint, there was surprisingly little following up of her work, and the history of women's work later in the nineteenth century remained for a long time unexplored by historians.[8] Recently the subject has been dealt with in a number of papers, monographs and general works. However, the study of the subject has revealed its complexity, and the difficulty of trying to look at work apart from other aspects of women's lives. The series of blue books on the employment of women and children in mines, factories and agriculture provide evidence of the nature of that work and of the care and compassion of the investigators. They also demonstrate the motivation of some of the concern shown. For the most part, and with one or two outstanding

NEEDLE MONEY.

Sweated Trades

Punch, *perhaps because its founders included Henry Mayhew, was always aware of the exploitation of sweated labour. In 1849 it printed the two cartoons above on opposite pages.*

exceptions, the humanitarians were not concerned with overwork, underpayment and exploitation generally. Sometimes they made specific denials of any interest in restricting hours or conditions for men and boys. Their concern with women and girls was not only with the physical but also with the moral environment, and side by side with condemnations of grossly over-strenuous and physically damaging work may be found comments on over- familiar relations between boy and girl workers, saucy and independent attitudes of young women and complaints of frivolous expenditure of their wages by young women on flashy clothes and jewelry.

PIN MONEY.

There were also complaints that factory girls were prevented from learning 'proper' domestic skills by going out to work, and from taking up the more suitably feminine occupation of domestic service. Restrictions placed on female labour were partly intended to reinforce the traditional role of women as managers of the home and family as well as to limit their exploitation.

The feminist movement which emerged in the latter half of the century was mainly made up of middle class women seeking equality of opportunity in work and education with men. For many such women the restrictions on female labour were seen as a limitation on equality of opportunity. Why shouldn't women work night shifts if they wished? Why should their hours be restricted when men were free to make whatever bargains they wished with their employers, based on industries and skills and not on sex or gender? Given the clearly paternalistic and discriminatory attitudes of many of the reformers towards women and their work, the case of the feminists seemed logical enough. Nevertheless, women, in any case at the bottom of the heap in most trades when it came to wages and terms of employment, clung pragmatically to protective legislation, whatever the motivation of its originators. This conflict between the political feminists and the working women represented by their trade unions accounts for some of the divisions in the women's movement of the later years of the century.[9] It also highlights the important point that there was little or no over-arching 'gender solidarity' during the nineteenth century. Problems and disabilities varied from class to class and could dictate opposing strategies. It also highlights the dangers in making too rigid a division between public and private worlds. For the working women, the conditions under which they worked were assessed in the light of a supposed set of standards of female behaviour and female family relations. The crucial public issues of wages and hours of work for men and women were evaluated and contested on the basis of assumptions about family responsibilities which might have been considered purely private. At the workplace and within the trade unions, the attempt by skilled men to restrict women to unskilled and low-paid jobs was based on the assumption that women, who rarely supported a dependent family, would always be prepared to undercut male skilled wages. The wives of the skilled workmen, whose hope of a regular income and space and time to care for their home and children depended on the maintenance of the men's wage-rates, could find themselves supporting male exclusiveness in the trades.

Men's work has been historically treated as an unproblematic concept, partly because the family background of nineteenth-century males has been taken as given. The history of labour organisations and of campaigns for improvement in hours, conditions and wages has been logged on the assumption that all workmen wanted shorter hours, a better working environment and higher wages. When it came to women workers, problems were seen. Women did not often form trade unions. When these were formed for them, as in the last years of the nineteenth century, by women reformers or by sympathetic men trade unionists, working women were often hesitant in their support and apathetic except in times of actual heightened conflict like strikes and lock-outs. Apologists explained women's problems — most working women were only occupied full-time in their jobs between school and marriage, their wage-rates were not a lifetime's concern; married women were usually doing two jobs if they worked full-time, as they had their homes to tend after work, so they had no time for meetings; women's wages were always low, so their subscriptions could not support a permanent organisation. All these things were of course true, but it might also have been suggested that the problem could lie not with the women, but with the unions. Like most nineteenth century institutions, trade unions had been started by men and had been built up to deal with men's working conditions. There is no reason why women, even full-time working women, should have the same problems at work as men, or should seek the same advantages from organisation. The structure of trade unions, from the cost of subscriptions and the method of collecting them, through the organisation and timing of meetings to the demands about hours, wages and conditions may have seemed largely irrelevant to women whose wages, whether they were married or not, were almost always seen as part of a family wage, and

18

whose needs may have been much more for flexibility of working hours, for a spacial and temporal arrangement that recognised the concern a woman had for her young children or siblings, even for more space for lavatories and washbasins at work rather than a slight increase in pay. What is more, women, far more than men, have very different patterns of needs in the various stages of their lives. Generalisations about 'women' often miss the enormous difference between an unmarried girl, a married woman with children and a widow with a grown-up family. It seems, then, that for the history of women's aspirations as workers we often have to look at episodes and informal organisations rather than a formal trade society.

The awareness of the interconnection of women's experiences in the family and the workplace has emerged with the growth of a history of society which is concerned to look beyond formal organisations and political structures and to take cognisance of other institutions and events which affect the lives of all people. Michael Anderson's pioneering study of family life in one industrial community based mainly on demographic statistics and census returns leaves open many questions, but his approach to work which starts from the family rather than from the factory clearly has a great deal of attraction for historians of women. Louise Tilly and Joan Scott's brief study, *Women Work and Family* draws together a great deal of the work that has been done on the European family, much of it on Britain, and makes an excellent beginning of a newer family-located study of women's work both inside and away from the home. A more recent study by Leonora Davidoff and Catherine Hall of a number of middle-class families in the early industrial period again brings out the crucial role played by family connections and family loyalties in the establishment of the trading and business concerns of early entrepreneurs.[10]

Generalisations, then, about women's work in the nineteenth century must still be treated with care. The connection between the work and the rewards of men and women was complex. Women were used as cheap labour, and the forcing down of men's wages by dilution of their trades disadvantaged their whole family, wives and children as well as husbands. The realisation that for the working people wages and working conditions were viewed from the point of view of the family rather than the individual has helped to bring some of the complexities of the social as well as the economic implications of work and wages into focus, but the mass of information that we need to understand the questions involved is still only being gradually produced. A good brief account of some of the most recent findings about women's work together with a useful short bibliography can be found in the introductory essay by Angela V. John to the volume of essays *Unequal Opportunities*, published in 1986.[11] Perhaps the most interesting work yet which takes full account of the insights of recent concern with the family is K.D.M. Snell's *Annals of the Labouring Poor* which demonstrates by close attention to contemporary records the changes in the family economy, and in particular the extent to which women contributed to the earning power of artisan and labouring families until the middle of the nineteenth century.[12]

When historians speak of 'work' they tend to mean paid work outside the home, or at least work which contributes directly to the production of goods or services beyond the subsistence needs of the household which may be sold to produce a family income. But for both sexes much of the actual work done every day has

always gone into the basic subsistence of the family. Child rearing, cleaning, the preparation of food and the maintenance of the home and garden, the clothes and shoes of the family, the provision of entertainment and instruction beyond what is available in the market place, the maintenance of social connections with family and friends beyond the immediate household — all these things take up a great percentage of the time and energy of people of all classes. As the nineteenth century progressed and gender roles in all classes seem to have become more clearly differentiated, more and more of this non-waged work seems to have been allocated to the women.

In all classes a well-run home clearly contributed to the well-being of all. Among the very poorest the struggle was greatest and the effects of good management probably the most telling. The life of the women of the poorest strata in the towns and cities has been

Domestic Servants

Throughout the nineteenth century the job that employed most women was that of domestic service. Servants were hard-worked, dependent and subject to every kind of exploitation — including sexual exploitation — by their employers. The idealisation of women did not extend to these women and girls, who were expected to carry coal, clean fireplaces and domestic boilers and empty slops for wages which could often be reckoned in pence per week rather than shillings.

*Servants varied from the single maid-of-all-work like the little maid in Dickens' **Old Curiosity Shop** to members of large staffs in grand houses and hotels like the parlourmaids in the photograph.*

the most difficult to recover, indeed it is mainly from the memories of those who were still living when the new interest developed that we can get any but the barest record. Many surveys were made by journalists and others towards the end of the century. Some

of these were informed by sympathy and concern, but very few were able to speak for the urban or rural poor. Even sympathetic outsiders could be repelled by the poorest slum-dwellers, whose children George Gissing described as 'bald, red-eyed, doughy-limbed abortions ... hapless spawn of diseased humanity, born to embitter and brutalise yet further the lot of those who unwillingly gave them life'. The techniques of recovery developed by the use of interviews and oral evidence have been able to fill out somewhat the evidence of observers and official reports, and to give us some picture of the vital role played by women in holding together the fragile economic, social and emotional structure of the working class family. A valuable drawing together of much of this evidence, enriched by oral and other material from his native Birmingham, is in Carl Chinn's *They Worked All Their Lives*, which also contains a useful bibliography of material after 1880.[13] Among all classes women contributed to family life by their work at home and by their earnings outside the home. Apart from the exceptional case of the textile factory districts, the wages of unmarried girls rarely covered their keep, and were regarded as a contribution to the family income rather than the basis for any kind of independent life.

The organisation of the household economy imposed different burdens on the women of different classes. Many women of the higher classes were undoubtedly bored, under-employed and socially restricted. Nevertheless, the business of running a household even with the help of servants was demanding enough, while the importance of maintaining connections with all members of the family and a circle of friends and acquaintances was not only of social and emotional importance, but also of the greatest economic importance. Family connections were all-important in the development of business and trade, while for most of the century the chance of well-paid and prestigious employment for a young man or of a good marriage for a young woman depended as much on who you knew as on who you were. The social round in which women engaged was thus by no means purely frivolous. At the top of the pyramid was Queen Victoria with her nine children and thirty-six grandchildren, constantly concerned with their health and behaviour, with their careers and their marriages. At every level of society from the queen downward women were similarly occupied in their own social group and their own family concerns.[14]

Politics and the Law

For all the legal superiority of the man as head of the family, there can be no doubt that many women shared the actual responsibilities and often made decisions of the greatest importance. Outside the home women of good social standing and some property also exercised a considerable degree of authority over the poor of both sexes through their concern with charity. As the century progressed, however, the nature of charitable activity changed. In the early years the wife of the squire or the parson could certainly rule the village, if she so desired, by a variety of strategies from the running of the school to the distribution of soup and blankets to the deserving aged. As the nineteenth century developed, however, and the bulk of the population moved into towns and cities, more and more of the social functions of charitable activity were taken over either by large concerns, including the Charity Organisation Society, founded in 1870 to coordinate charitable work and to employ professional or expert administrators, or by local government. Ladies wishing to work for charity were increasingly directed into money-raising by social events or subscription, a form of activity which did not appeal to all. Some philanthropically-minded women therefore directed their energies into local government.

As Patricia Hollis has shown in her recent study — the first full treatment of the subject — women gained the vote in local elections half a century before they gained the parliamentary franchise.[15] The right of women ratepayers to vote for local councillors, school board members and poor law guardians was established in a series of measures beginning in 1869 and continuing into the twentieth century. As each new act or legal decision opened up more space for women as electors and as members of these local administrative bodies, their presence began to affect the institutions concerned, even though by the end of the nineteenth century they only represented a tiny minority on most of the controlling committees. Patricia Hollis stresses the humanising effect of the presence even of so few women. The charitable concern for the welfare of the poor and disadvantaged which had motivated earlier generations of socially aware ladies was reborn in the more formal atmosphere of local government. It can also be argued that the moral standards and the moral judgements of earlier charitable administration were to some degree transmitted into the welfare work of many of these latter-day organisations. It is certainly a fact that, although by the end of the century a small number of working men from very poor backgrounds had gained admission to the charmed circle of local government, and had even entered Parliament, no woman of the working class was to take any part in the political system at any level until well into the twentieth century. It is another illustration of the concentration by most of our historians on the highest level of national politics, that the story of women in local government has waited so long for its historian. The main works on nineteenth century municipal politics make no mention of women as electors, candidates or subjects of local administration, although the areas of poor law provision, housing and education have always been of as great or greater concern to women as to men. Those working men who had been elected to some local councils in the later decades of the century were seen, except in a very few I.L.P. strongholds, as spokesmen for 'labour' in its most limited sense, and contributed on questions of wages and employment conditions rather than on the wider issues of welfare. Of neither sex can it be said that a representative working-class voice was heard in local government by the end of the nineteenth century. To the extent that there was a women's presence, this presence was still that of the charitable and philanthropic middle or upper class lady, and not that of the working woman or working class mother.

The power to make decisions about one's own and other people's lives is one of the measures of authority in society. There is no doubt that most women in the nineteenth century had less power of this kind than men of their own rank and station. It is also clear that rich women had more power and authority than poor men, and that many poor men's lives were controlled by the decisions of women employers, social and charitable workers or, in the case of tradesmen, customers. In politics, as long as open voting persisted, that is until the ballot act of 1872, the influence of wealthy, propertied women could have more effect on the voting behaviour of shopkeepers and small property owners than they could have exercised by their own vote given in a secret ballot. In any case, political power for most of the nineteenth century resided more with the distributors of patronage than in the electors. It was the increasing importance given to voting, both as part of the development of a modern party system in Parliament and as an indication of citizenship that led to the demand for women's suffrage in the second half of the century. It is worth recalling, however, that the admission of the poorest sections of the population to the political realm was hardly more rapid than the admission of women. In a century in which status was closely related to property, the question of property rights was closely connected with questions of political rights and political status.

Throughout the century an unmarried woman — legally known as feme sole — had property rights which were in most ways the same as those of a man. She could inherit and bequeath property, sell or give away property on which there was no legal restriction and engage in all kinds of commercial transactions in exactly the same way as a man. Prejudice might work against her when she looked for credit, but there is little evidence to suggest that a woman with clear title to property was disadvantaged by her gender in dealing with it. The matter was, however, very different for a married woman or *feme covert*. Most women in nineteenth century Britain married — one estimate suggests as many as 94 per cent of those who reached marriageable age. For these women, at least for those comparatively few among them who belonged to the propertied classes, the laws that mattered were those relating to married women's property. Even prior to these were the laws and customs which concerned marriage itself.

Although the nineteenth century may have seen an increase in the proportion of people who married in parts of Britain, the statistics of numbers of marriages, age of partners at marriage, length of marriages as well as the customs by which marriage vows were exchanged and marriages recognised varied very greatly from region to region.[16] For most of the century Britain, although sharing most of the institutions of government and a unified economy, was still an area of marked national and regional differences. It was in such traditional and familial matters as marriage customs that some of the greatest variations existed. For one thing there were great regional differences in the distribution of churches, religious groups and sects. The largely Catholic Irish and the largely dissenting Protestant Welsh differed very greatly in such matters from the areas in which the Church of England was dominant. But even in the areas with

no dominant dissenting groups there were many people who did not attend the established church or accept its rituals and control. There was no civil marriage until 1837, nor was there legal recognition before that date of services carried out in any but Anglican churches, with the exception of those performed by Quakers and Jews. Since the middle of the eighteenth century, with those two exceptions, only marriages carried out in church by an ordained clergyman, after the publishing of banns on three successive Sundays or after the purchase of a licence from a bishop to marry without banns, had been recognised as valid in law. The introduction of civil marriage in 1837 removed some of the restrictions, and the same act saw the extension of licence to conduct wedding services to nonconformist churches. Nevertheless, after 1837 as well as before it is clear that a great number of marriages were solemnised in informal ways from the exchange of vows before witnesses (sufficient in Scotland for a legal bond until 1857) to ceremonies like the various versions of beesom or 'over the broom' weddings in which a union was created by jumping over a broom propped across the house threshold. In the latter case the couple could be divorced by reversing the ceremony, an easier process than the more ritualised form of popular divorce which was represented by the wife sale. Historians of popular mores have begun to examine these customs, which remained in general outside the law courts, because they took place among those classes for whom issues of property were of little concern.[17] One area though in which marriage customs and property did very much affect the poorer women was the question of bastardy. Before the 1834 Poor Law Amendment Act a pregnant woman could swear a claim against the putative father of her child. Unless he could refute the allegation, he was obliged either to marry her or to contribute to the child's maintenance. The 1834 Act placed the full responsibility for the children born out of wedlock on the mother; if the father could be proved to be such in court, the poor law authorities could force him to pay for the child's support in the workhouse, but no money was to go directly to the mother. The idea of the law's framers was that this shift of responsibility to the mother would act as a deterrent to extra-marital sex, but, as Ursula Henriques showed in an important article some years ago, far from having this effect, the Act increased illegitimacy and infanticide and provoked such widespread anger in many parts of the country and among many different sections of the population in the ten years following its enactment, that it was eventually very considerably modified.[18] An interesting thing about the response to the 1834 proposals was that in some districts, such as south Wales, local spokesmen, including clergymen, defended traditional courting and marriage customs, which clearly included pre-marital sex, as reasonable and acceptable. The new proposals disturbed traditional practices by tempting young men to avoid their responsibilities and so disrupted a system which had hitherto been socially acceptable and reasonably fair to both men and women. The century saw the regularisation of marriage customs and the dying out of some local and class-specific forms. Whether the position of women within marriage among the poorer classes was better for this greater regularity is, however, very unclear.

For women of the higher classes, marriage was indissolubly mixed with property. For the record of this we have a mass of family legal documents, court cases, private acts of Parliament and manuscript and literary evidence. Demands which arose in the second half of the century for the reform of the law relating to married women's property were mainly motivated by injustices imposed by the laws governing the status of *feme covert* as these affected men and women of the middle classes in society. As the great jurist A.V. Dicey observed, in the early part of the century 'the daughters of the wealthy were .... protected under the rules of equity in the enjoyment of their separate property. The daughters of working men possessed little propety of their own.'[19] Legal cases had been fought in the eighteenth century over questions of pin money — the allocation by contract to a wife of a regular allowance for personal expenses — and over wives' separate property. By the use of entail, strict settlement and jointure landed families were able to guarantee their daughters, even when married and under the law of coverture, access to land and money which could not be alienated by their husbands. Under common law, until the Dower Act of 1833, widows were entitled to a third of their former husband's real estate property, but among the wealthy this provision had become obsolete, to be replaced by agreed jointures to be administered on the widows' behalf by trustees. Family papers show that some provision for separate property for daughters on marriage was almost universal among the rich. Family records also show that, whatever the exact legal position, most women among the commercial and gentry classes who brought money into a marriage retained control over all or part of it. Cases such as the famous one of Caroline Norton in the 1830s, in which even her earnings from writing after her separation from her husband were held to be his property, do not necessarily illustrate the generally-held attitudes among the moderately wealthy. One of the famous examples of the inequity of the law is Mrs Fawcett's account of being robbed of her purse. When she attended court to give evidence against the thief, she heard him accused of the theft of a purse, 'the property of Henry Fawcett'.

*More gaily-dressed ladies of light morals in a detail from Phoebus Levine's **Cremorne Gardens** (1864).*

Naturally she was angry, but it is worth noticing that this was the first time she seems to have been aware of her husband's legal ownership — in other words, in a happy marriage as hers was, her right to spend as she wished had not been questioned.[20] This is not to suggest that the establishment of the right of married women to own money and property in their own right was not an important victory for women, but simply to suggest that the rigours of legal absolutes may have been experienced only in situations of conflict. The recognition of the right of married women to own property was established by a series of acts which have been listed by Lee Holcombe in her recent book on the subject. These acts also limited the extent to which husbands were responsible for debts incurred by their wives, and there is some suggestion in the debates in parliament which were concerned with these issues that the law of coverture could be onerous to men of small and

medium property as well as to their wives. By the end of the century women were more secure in their ownership of property and could incur debts and sue in their own names, even when married.

Marriage laws and customs changed in certain fundamental ways during the century, and again the changes affected different classes in different ways. As with the question of married women's property, the laws relating to divorce had always borne more heavily on those of moderate or slender means. For the rich of any denomination, an annulment or a divorce obtained by private Act of Parliament permitted the dissolution of a marriage. For those who had gone through an informal ceremony or none, of course, there were no legal prohibitions to a divorce. For the majority of the population, however, there was no escape from a marriage once entered into, before the middle of the century.

ct of 1857 allowed a spouse to
r divorce in the courts if the
spouse behaved in certain
:ptable ways. A husband could
sue for divorce from a wife who could
be proved to have committed adultery.
A wife could sue only if the husband
had compounded his adultery by other
misdemeanours such as cruelty. The
law, which was in any case available
only to those whose purses were long
enough to bear the not inconsiderable
costs of a law case, was weighted
heavily against women. Not only were
the grounds for divorce more difficult
for a woman to establish, but also,
given the law of coverture, a woman in
a situation of conflict was far less likely
to have the independent resources to
proceed against her husband. So far
from increasing the possibility for most
women of escaping from the trap of an
unhappy marriage, the divorce
legislation with its almost inevitable
awarding of custody of the children of
the marriage to the father, highlighted
the extent to which women were
regarded as junior partners in marriage.
The act of 1857 also retained the
concept of damages to be awarded to a
husband for loss of his wife. This
financial assessment of the worth of a
wife's services had existed in law for
many years. Under the concept of
'criminal conversation' it had for many
years been possible for a husband to
sue his wife's lover for financial
compensation for the alienation of her
affections and the loss of his conjugal
rights. The higher the social status of
the couple, the greater the
compensation awarded to the deprived
husband. No such compensation was
available to an injured wife.[21]

The whole question of the double
standard of sexual and marital
behaviour which was expected of men
and women is one of the central
questions of nineteenth century
history. From the earliest years debates
in parliament, journals and fiction
writers — including some of the

world's greatest novelists — reverted
to the idea that standards of behaviour
were basically different for men and
women. For all the improvement in the
legal status of women within marriage
that had occurred by the end of the
nineteenth century, this distinction
remained, demonstrated by the law
concerning divorce and the custody of
children and by the general public
attitude. It was, for example, regarded
as scandalous to suggest that Queen
Victoria, a widow with no obligations
of marital fidelity, had had sexual
relations with her confidential servant,
John Brown, in the 1860s and '70s,
while the flagrant sexual infidelities of
her son, later Edward VII, were looked
on with tolerance and amusement.[22]

A historian looking at the history of
women is likely to fall into one
dangerous trap. Events, trends,
campaigns and issues which are
articulated as being 'women's issues'
tend to stand out and to offer
themselves as the proper subject of
study. In fact, of course, many of the
questions in any generation which
most urgently concern women are
likely to be those which also concern
men. Women's part in social and
political movements of which they are
not the only — or even the primary —
initiators may well be overlooked, and
their experience and influence thereby
underestimated. In my own work I
have found that women's presence in
the popular movements of the early
nineteenth century has been seriously
underestimated and under-reported.

*There could hardly have been a greater
contrast with the fine clothes of the
prostitutes than the working garb of the Pit
Brow Lasses who worked sorting coal at the
top of coal mines. A campaign to exclude all
women from colliery work, even at the
surface, brought them into the public eye in
the late 60s, and the popularity of picture
postcards of the trousered figures shows that
Munby was not alone in being fascinated by
them.*

Talk with Eliza Hayes, aged 25,
a Row Bridge.

Eliza: "A've niver done nowt else but this work, all t' days
o' ma life."

Recent work on food riots and on the Highland clearances has restored women to their place in movements which were inspired by class or national feelings rather than by gender.[23] In the later nineteenth century it is clear that many women socialists regarded the achievement of universal suffrage as being of prior importance to the achievement of women's suffrage on the same property qualification as men's. The women's suffrage campaign was dominated by women, the early labour movement mainly by men, but the number of women involved in the labour movement should not be underestimated.

The subject of sexual mores is one in which a purely female approach is also likely to be confusing. One of the most significant changes in the nineteenth century was the fall in the birth rate. There were strong feminist arguments in support of women's right to control her body and to choose how often she had sex with her

be against the feminist influence as a determining factor. In world experience a declining birth rate has generally accompanied a rising standard of living and in particular an improvement in the legal and social position of women. The exact mechanism by which these factors combine is still debated.

On the wider question of nineteenth century sexual mores there is still some debate. One of the first results of the more liberal literary atmosphere of the 1960s was the publication of Stephen Marcus' *The Other Victorians*. Based to a great extent on a hitherto suppressed book, *My Secret Life* by 'Walter', *The Other Victorians* revealed a secret world of sexual exploitation and dominion by wealthy Victorian men over poor women and girls, including servants and working-class children. Marcus quoted the authority of William Acton, whose volume on *Prostitution*, first published in 1857 has since been reprinted and widely used as an authoritative account of Victorian attitudes to sex. Acton is best known for his assertion that genteel women do not get pleasure from sex, and for his massive assessment of the number of prostitutes in London. The picture that emerged was one of a society polarised between demure, frigid women and rapacious lustful men whose desires were catered for by a wide net of professional and semi-professional prostitutes motivated entirely by the need to earn money. Stephen Marcus is a literary critic and not a historian. His examination of the male fantasies in *My Secret Life* and some other texts is fascinating and revealing. There is however great danger in taking such works as literal accounts of life. Walter's tally reaches

husband and how many children she should have. However, there is no proof that the various feminist campaigns were influential in affecting the sex life of Victorian men and women. Methods of birth control had been known for many years, and we have absolutely no evidence as to whether the fall in the birth rate resulted from sexual abstinence, the use of contraceptive devices or the resort to abortion. The probability, judging from the social classes in which the decline occurred, seems to unbelievable lengths and, as Professor F.B. Smith has pointed out, is extremely vague in important matters of detail.[24] Some of the extreme pictures of sexual exploitation and male dominance may have been fictitious or quite untypical. Prostitution did of course exist on a large scale in British cities, and the gruesome episode of the 'Ripper' murders of five prostitutes in 1888 helped to revive concern with the squalor of late-Victorian city life. There were a number of occasions during the century in which the issue of prostitution became a public one and was widely discussed in the press, including the campaign against the Contagious Diseases Acts of the 1860s which attempted to introduce registration and regular medical examination of prostitutes, and the sensational disclosures of child prostitution made by W.T. Stead in 1885. Emphasis on the cruel and exploitative elements in the relations between the sexes, while clearly necessary to gain reform and protection, may still have preserved a distorted view of the generality of sexual relations. As Tolstoy noted, harmonious families resemble one another and are not very interesting to outsiders, and evidence from memoirs and biographies, as well as from unpublished sources which had tended to be suppressed by earlier writers, such as the correspondence of Charles and Fanny Kingsley, have for some time been offering a more balanced view.[25] Nevertheless, double standards continued to be applied to the sexual behaviour of men and women, from the highest in the land downwards, and by the end of the century very little had been achieved either by the Social Purity crusade which attempted to impose stricter standards of sexual behaviour on men, or by the daring new women who attempted to widen the areas of accepted sexual behaviour for women. The politics of sexual relations remained confused and elusive.

Conclusion

The history of nineteenth century British women is the story of millions of people, members of different classes, different nationalities and different beliefs. Generalisations about so many people over so long a period must be suspect and very tentative. British coins had a woman on either side for most of the century — Britannia and Victoria — and British women were regarded abroad as courageous travellers, bossy governesses and managing memsahibs. Britain's industrial supremacy would have been impossible without women and child workers. Population expansion, industrialisation and urbanisation which changed the structure of British society affected women in their family and working roles, but the changes that took place in the size of families, in the authority which women of all classes exercised in their families and in the wider community cannot be parallelled exactly with the economic and political changes. The histories of the family and of the customs connected with it, marriage, sexual relations, child-rearing and education are histories which are more difficult to recover or to confine within precise dates. Interesting and exciting work is being done in some of these areas, and the modern concern with woman's place in society will ensure that all social history will now take account of both sexes.

Notes

[1] Most of the recent work has been done on the early 20th century when the final confrontations took place. **Ray Strachey's** *The Cause* first published in 1912 remains an excellent 'committed' account of the nineteenth century movement.

Brian Harrison, *Separate Spheres : the Opposition to Women's Suffrage in Britain* (1978) for the other side.

[2] A useful bibliography with explanatory notes covering most of the nineteenth century is **S. Barbara Kanner** 'The women of England in a century of social change, 1815-1914. A select bibliography'. Part 1 in (ed.) **M. Vicinus** *Suffer and be Still: Women in the Victorian Age* (Bloomington and London 1972); Part 11 in (ed.) **M. Vicinus,** *A Widening Sphere. Changing Roles of Victorian Women* (Bloomington and London 1977). This, of course, only goes up to the mid-1970s. A fuller three-volume bibliography *Women in English Social History 1800-1914* by the same author was published by Garland (New York) in 1987. For a bibliography of Irish women, see **Anna Brady,** *Women in Ireland* (1987).

[3] For a discussion of some of the problems involved in the term, see **Sheila Rowbotham,** 'The trouble with Patriarchy', first printed in the *New Statesman*, 21-28 December 1979, and re-printed in the author's collection of essays, *Dreams and Dilemmas* (1983). The volume also contains a section on 'History', pp 162-208, in which a number of the questions raised by the influence of contemporary feminism are discussed as part of the experience of a feminist historian.

[4] For a fuller discussion of the concept of gender, see, **Ivan Illich,** *Gender* (New York 1982).

[5] **Jean Bethke Elshtain,** *Public Man, Private Woman: Women in Social and Political Thought* (Oxford 1981). For a sympathetic and sensitive account of the doctrines of separate spheres as expounded by Hannah More and experienced in the lives of some middle-class English families, see **Leonora Davidoff** and **Catherine Hall,** *Family Fortunes* (1987).

[6] Queen Victoria must have a claim to be the best-documented figure in history. As well as numerous biographies and hagiographies large selections of her letters, journals and sketch-books have been published, as well as countless reminiscences and biographies of those who had any association with her. She is, by any standards, a fascinating figure. The best and most readable biography remains that by **Elizabeth Longford,** *Victoria R.I* (London, Weidenfeld and Nicholson 1964). Later works have added a few additional items of information, but

have not significantly altered Lady Longford's picture. There has not yet been much consideration of the effect of the long tenure of this top job by a woman on her female subjects, or indeed of the role of gender in her influence and shaping of the monarchy. But see my *Queen Victoria, Gender and Power* (1990) for a short consideration of some of the questions involved.

[7] There were very many surveys in the late nineteenth and early twentieth centuries. In the middle of the nineteenth century **Henry Mayhew's** investigations on behalf of the *Morning Chronicle* gave unique insights into the lives of the men and women of the metropolis. Later, more 'scientific' surveys of London and York were made, **Henry Mayhew**, *London Labour and the London Poor* (1851); **E.P. Thompson** and **Eileen Yeo**, (eds.) *The Unknown Mayhew* (1971); **Charles Booth**, *Life and Labour of the People of London (1889)*; **B. Seebohm Rowntree**, *Poverty, a Study of Town Life* (1901). For one account of the lives of the rural poor, see **Flora Thompson**, *Lark Rise to Candleford (1939)*. For an interesting sample from various reports published in the second half of the century, **Peter Keating**, (ed.), *Into Unknown England 1866-1913: Selections from the Social Explorers* (1976).

[8] **Ivy Pinchbeck**, *Women Workers and the Industrial Revolution* (1st ed. 1930, repr. 1969).

[9] An interesting illustration of this division is described in **Rosemary Fuerer**, 'The meaning of 'sisterhood': the British Women's Movement and protective legislation, 1870-1900', *Victoran Studies*, 31 No 2, (Winter 1988), pp. 233-260.

[10] **Michael Anderson**, *Family Structure in Nineteenth Century Lancashire* (Cambridge 1971); **Louise A. Tilly** and **Joan W. Scott**, *Women, Work and Family* (1978); Davidoff and Hall, *op. cit.*

[11] **Angela V. John**, (ed.) *Unequal Opportunities: Women's Employment in England 1800-1918* (Oxford 1986).

[12] **K.D.M. Snell**, *Annals of the Labouring Poor* (Cambridge 1985).

[13] **Carl Chinn**, *They Worked all their Lives: Women of the Urban Poor in England, 1880-1939* (Manchester 1988).

[14] **Leonore Davidoff**, *The Best Circles; 'Society', Etiquette and the Season* (1973).

[15] **Patricia Hollis**, *Ladies Elect: Women in English Local Government 1865-1914* (Oxford 1987).

[16] An account of Irish marriage figures in the post-famine years, see **K.H. Connell** 'Catholicism and Marriage in the century after the Famine' in his *Irish Peasant Society* (Oxford 1968) pp 51-86.

[17] For a comprehensive view of British marriage customs, **John R. Gillis**, *For Better, For Worse: British Marriages 1600 to the present* (Oxford 1985). For wife-selling, see **E.P. Thompson** 'The Sale of Wives' in *Customs in Common* (1991) and **S.P. Menefee**, *Wives for Sale: an Ethnographic Study of British Popular Divorce* (New York 1981).

[18] **Ursula Henriques**, 'Bastardy and the New Poor Law' in *Past and Present*, No 37 (July 1967), pp 103-129.

[19] **A.V. Dicey**, *Law and Public Opinion in England* (first pub 1910, 2nd ed, 1962), p 384. For an account of the law relating to married women's property and the campaigns to change it, **Lee Holcombe**, *Wives and Property. Reform of the Married Women's Property Law in Nineteenth Century England* (Oxford 1983).

[20] **Millicent Fawcett**, *What I remember* (1924), p 62.

[21] **Susan Staves**, 'Money for Honor: Damages for Criminal Conversation' in

(ed) **Harry C. Payne**, *Studies in Eighteenth Century Culture* Vol 11 (Wisconsin 1982), pp 47-76.

[22] For John Brown see, **Tom Cullen**, *The Empress Brown: the Story of a Royal Friendship* (1969); for Edward VII, see any history of the period. Can it be a persistence of the double standard that has led to the re-naming of Alexandra Road in North London as 'Langtry Parade' and of the local pub 'The Princess of Wales', as 'The Lily Langtry'?

[23] **E.P. Thompson**, 'The Moral Economy of the English Crowd', *Past and Present*, 50 (Feb 1971), pp 76-136. **Dorothy Thompson**, *The Chartists* (1984). **Malcolm I. Thomis** and **Jennifer Grimmet**, *Women in Protest 1800-1850* (1982).

[24] **Stephen Marcus**, *The Other Victorians* (1966). **F. Barry Smith**, 'Sexuality in Britain 1800-1900, some suggested Revisions' in **Martha Vicinus** (ed), *A Widening Sphere, Changing Roles of Victorian Women* (Indiana 1977), pp 182-198.

[25] **Susan Chitty**, *The Beast and the Monk* (1974).

[26] For a discussion of some of the ideas in this area of women at the very end of the century, see **Lucy Bland**, 'The Married woman, the 'New Woman' and the Feminist: Sexual Politics of the 1890's', in **Jane Rendall**, *Equal or Different, Women's Politics 1800-1914* (1987), pp 141-164.

Further Reading

[1] The enormous range of the subject means that any short selection of essential reading must be inadequate. Again I refer to the bibliographies given in note 2.

Primary sources have also been left out in the main, although many are accessible and interesting. The literature of the century abounds in insights, perhaps the most valuable of all, and many studies have been done of women in the nineteenth century based entirely on literary sources. These have been omitted for reasons of space, since it would seem to be invidious to suggest only one or two from among so many.

All the books mentioned in the notes to the text are recommended. Those listed below are important works that have not been mentioned in the notes.

1. Work

There are separate monographs on a number of trades. Three studies which cover important and under-studied subjects are Pamela Horn, *The Rise and Fall of the Victorian Servant* (1875); Patricia Malcomson, *English Laundresses, a Social History* (Illinois, 1986); Duncan Bythell, *The Sweated Trades : Outwork in Nineteenth-Century Britain* (New York 1978). For an excellent recent study of gender and work in the Nineteenth-century British textile industry and a serious examination of the theoretical questions involved, Sonya O. Rose, *Limited Livelihoods: Gender and Class in Nineteenth-Century England,* (University of California Press 1992).

2. Trade Unionism

Sheila Lewenhak, *Women and Trade Unions* (1977); N.C. Soldon, *Women in British Trade Unions 1874-1976* (Dublin 1978),

3. Family

For the Irish in London, Lynn Hollen Lees, *Exiles of Erin: Irish Migrants in Victorian London* (Manchester 1979); Brian Harrison, 'Women's Health and the Women's Movement in Britain 1840-1940' in Charles Webster, (ed) *Biology, Medicine and Society* (Cambridge 1981); O.R. McGregor, *Divorce in England* (1957); G. Rubin and David Sugarman, (eds) *Law, Economy and Society: Essays in the History of English Law 1750-1914* (Oxford 1984); Angus McLaren, *Birth Control in Nineteenth-Century England (1978).*

4. Sexual mores and prostitution

Brian Harrison, 'Underneath the Victorians', *Victorian Studies* X (1967) pp 239-262, Judith R. Walkowitz, *Prostitution and Victorian Society: Women Class and the State* (Cambridge 1980),

5. General

Jane Rendal, *The Origins of Modern Feminism: Women in Britain, France and the U.S. 1780-1860* (1985); David Rubinstein, *Before the Suffragettes* (Brighton, 1986), and for a short, clearly-written account which places the British experience within a wider world picture, Sheila Rowbotham, *Women in Movement: Feminism and Social Action* (1992).